Pebble® Plus

Celebrating Differences

T0045139

We All Look Different

by Melissa Higgins

Consulting Editor: Gail Saunders-Smith, PhD

Consultant: Donna Barkman
Children's Literature Specialist and Diversity Consultant
Ossining, New York

CAPSTONE PRESS
a capstone imprint

Pebble Plus is published by Capstone Press,
1710 Roe Crest Drive, North Mankato, Minnesota 56003.
www.capstonepub.com

Copyright © 2012 by Capstone Press, a Capstone imprint. All rights reserved.
No part of this publication may be reproduced in whole or in part, or stored in a retrieval system, or transmitted in any form or by any means, electronic, mechanical, photocopying, recording, or otherwise, without written permission of the publisher. For information regarding permission, write to Capstone Press,
1710 Roe Crest Drive, North Mankato, Minnesota 56003.

Library of Congress Cataloging-in-Publication Data
Higgins, Melissa
We all look different / by Melissa Higgins.
p. cm.—(Pebble Plus. Celebrating differences)
Includes bibliographical references and index.
Summary: "Simple text and full-color photos celebrate differences in appearances"—Provided by publisher.
ISBN 978-1-4296-7576-5 (library binding)—ISBN 978-1-4296-7890-2 (paperback)
1. Individual differences in children—Juvenile literature. 2. Individual differences—Juvenile literature. 3. Human physiology—Juvenile literature. I. Title.

BF723.I56H54 2012
155.2'2—dc23 2011036743

Editorial Credits
Jeni Wittrock, editor; Gene Bentdahl, designer; Svetlana Zhurkin, media researcher; Kathy McColley, production specialist; Marcy Morin, studio scheduler; Sarah Schuette, photo stylist

Photo Credits
Capstone Studio: Karon Dubke, cover; Dreamstime: James Blinn, 9; Getty Images: Johner Images, 19; iStockphoto: Aldo Murillo, 20–21, Blend Images, 7, Daniel Laflor, 5, Nina Shannon, 1; Shutterstock: Distinctive Images, 15, GWImages, 17, Monkey Business Images, 10–11, Rob Hainer, 13

Note to Parents and Teachers

The Celebrating Differences series supports national social studies standards related to individual development and identity. This book describes and illustrates differences in appearance. The images support early readers in understanding the text. The repetition of words and phrases helps early readers learn new words. This book also introduces early readers to subject-specific vocabulary words, which are defined in the Glossary section. Early readers may need assistance to read some words and to use the Table of Contents, Glossary, Read More, Internet Sites, and Index sections of the book.

Printed in the United States 5692

Table of Contents

I Like How I Look 4
We Look Different 6
We Dress Differently 14
We Like Being Different . . . 20

Glossary 22
Read More 23
Internet Sites 23
Index 24

I Like How I Look

How we look is one thing that makes you, *you*—and me, *me*. I like who I am. I like the things that make me unique.

We Look Different

My friends have cinnamon skin,
peach skin, and chocolate skin.
We are all shapes and sizes.

Summer is our favorite time of year. The sun gives us more freckle power!

My hair is curly and yours is straight. We both like going to the library.

I am short and quick. I am
the fastest runner on my team.

We Dress Differently

The things I wear tell a story
about me. Orange is sunny
and happy, just like me.

My glasses help me see.
Grandma says my glasses
are picture frames for
my shining, brown eyes.

My braces help me get into the game. I love to play and practice hard.

We Like Being Different

Differences make life interesting. We are each one of a kind.

Glossary

brace—a frame worn around part of your body to support it

frame—a border that surrounds something, like a picture frame

freckle—a small, light brown spot on a person's skin

unique—one of a kind

Read More

Fox, Mem. *Whoever You Are.* San Diego: Harcourt Brace, 2006.

Parr, Todd. *It's Okay to Be Different.* New York: Little, Brown Books for Young Readers, 2009.

Tyler, Michael. *The Skin You Live In.* Chicago: Chicago Children's Museum, 2005.

Internet Sites

FactHound offers a safe, fun way to find Internet sites related to this book. All of the sites on FactHound have been researched by our staff.

Here's all you do:

Visit *www.facthound.com*

Type in this code: 9781429675765

Index

braces, 18
clothing, 14
eyes, 16
freckles, 8
glasses, 16
hair, 10
height, 12
shapes, 6
sizes, 6
skin, 6
speed, 12

Word Count: 144
Grade: 1
Early-Intervention Level: 17